ABERDEEN
SINCE
1900

PAUL HARRIS

LOMOND BOOKS

This edition first published by Lomond Books,
Granton, Edinburgh 1996

Originally published 1988 by Archive Publications
Reprinted 1998 by Lomond Books

© Copyright text and arrangement Paul Harris 1996
Photographs © Copyright Aberdeen Journals Ltd. and contributors
(see Acknowledgements) 1988, 1996
ISBN 0 947782 27 3

1.   *Overleaf:* bygone Aberdeen. Virginia Street in the 1950s.

2.   *Above:* Aberdeen Harbour, 1983. The Upper Dock with oil rig supply vessels and Salvesen House *(left).*

CONTENTS

ACKNOWLEDGEMENTS

PREFACE
by Lord Provost Henry E. Rae (1984-88)

INTRODUCTION 4—12

SELECT BIBLIOGRAPHY

DAWN OF A NEW
CENTURY 13—44

GETTING AROUND 45—77

AT WORK 78—120

DRAMA & SCANDAL! 121—147

AT PLAY 148—199

THE CHANGING FACE OF ABERDEEN 200—238

DIAL 999! 239—264

ACKNOWLEDGEMENTS

My thanks to all those who helped with this book and especially those at *The Press & Journal* including Harry Roulston, Editor, Tommy Forsyth in the library, who fielded all my requests and queries, and Sandy Smith who made excellent prints from the newspaper's store of glass plates. All the photographs here came from the files of Aberdeen Journals Ltd except where noted below. Thank you also to Geddes Wood and Ian Young of Scotpix, Aberdeen, for the loan of their fascinating cuttings books and for photographs numbered 112, 122, 129, 145, 173, 183, 197, 198 and 247. Other photographs are from the following sources: City of Aberdeen press office 3, Grampian Television 58, the late Douglas Dunn 135, Paul Harris 67.
Thank you also to Aberdeen City Libraries and George Moffat, City of Aberdeen Press Officer. And, last but by no means least, my thanks to Lord Provost Henry E. Rae for his support and encouragement.
I am delighted to see the publication of a new edition in 1996 as copies of the first printing have long since been exhausted.

Paul Harris
June 1996

PREFACE to 1988 edition

3.   Lord Provost Henry E. Rae (1984—88).

This could well be called a trip down memory lane with a difference, for it illustrates the gradual development of the City only in this century.

I do think, however, that it aptly portrays the spirit of the times and, perhaps even more important, the distinct charm and character of the City.

We can witness the gradual acceleration in the volume of traffic from the early years of this century to the almost unmanageable levels of today. Many of these old photographs also show the great and lively interest aroused in and around public events.

We can also see that in the 1930s Aberdeen was being developed at a fairly modest rate of progress. This was followed by the debacle of the war years, which left the City with massive housing problems.

We then witness the tremendous boom both in housing and in commercial development as Aberdeen changed rapidly and took a tremendous leap forward in the post-war years.

With the outbreak of typhoid in the mid 1960s, the City not only managed to contain the epidemic, but also, when it was over, regained its share and volume of trade and began again to successfully promote itself as one of the major centres of tourism in the country.

In essence, I think this more than anything else illustrates the resilience and resourcefulness of the City and its people in times of adversity.

This was followed by the advent of North Sea Oil and all the pressures this major development placed at all levels of activity within the City. Yet, despite these enormous demands on the infrastructure of the City, as this book clearly indicates, we were able to retain the basic character and the dignity of this ancient City of which we are all so immensely proud.

Lord Provost Henry E. Rae

INTRODUCTION

I was relatively new to Aberdeen in 1970 when the late Fenton Wyness, local historian, architect and savagely shrewd critic, introduced me to the changes being wrought in the City. We walked and worked together for some six months and the result was a collection of before and after photographs, *Aberdeen: Century of Change* (1971). Tony was, of course, an unremitting critic of the architectural changes in his native city and at times, indeed, his views bordered positively on the jaundiced. Nevertheless, and most importantly, he cared very much about the preservation of the city of Bon Accord.

I remember standing with him one chilly afternoon in the Netherkirkgate as he disdainfully prodded with his foot a plaque marking where the Wallace Tower once stood. I had always wondered about his apparent aversion to Marks & Spencers which, it was to turn out, was nothing to do with the goods on sale but related to the actual building.

"Progress!" he declared, and went on with the words, he was to repeat in the book. "To anyone who has lived in Aberdeen for the past fifty years it is obvious that the proverb 'Better say here it is, than here it was' is either unknown or carries very little weight".

Undoubtedly, Aberdeen has lost many fine buildings and I think Tony was correct in his concern. Nevertheless, the Wallace Tower was, at some effort and not inconsiderable expense, taken down stone by stone and re-erected at Tillydrone (224). It was probably not the best example. The fate of other buildings has been less happy. The Union Street premises of the Royal Northern Club, torn down to make way for a shopping development (223) in a quite extraordinary parallel to the wanton destruction of the New Club building in Edinburgh's Princes Streeet. Then there was the widely lamented demolition of the New Market (227) which so inflamed Sir John Betjeman. And the wholesale destruction of the slum areas of the Guestrow and Gallowgate (213), which, again, was something of a parallel with Edinburgh's destruction of the architecturally imposing but evil and smelly red light area of St. James's Square. Add to this the loss of assorted hotels, cinemas and places of entertainment, all overtaken by changing fashions in leisure and lifestyle.

It is important to recognise, however, that Aberdeen does not stand alone in having made these sort of changes: they are mirrored in most of the cities of Britain and the old buildings summarily removed have been replaced by ones of, let us say, variable quality. Tony was surer. For him, it was all part of a levelling out process which he termed "uniformity with mediocrity". He thought that what he regarded as "bad manners" in building were the by-products of commercial aggression and resulted

4.   Union Street in the fog of the days before Clean Air Acts.

5. *St. Clair* enters Aberdeen Harbour in heavy weather en route from Lerwick. The last steamship operated by the North of Scotland Orkney & Shetland Steamship Co., she made her final voyage on March 1st, 1967.

6. Waves batter the walls of the houses at the fishing village of Footdee ("Fittie").

in "architectural gimmickry". Without a doubt, his admonitory stance did make many in Aberdeen think again and it did contribute towards a generally more aware and enlightened attitude to the preservation of the past which gradually came about in the mid 1970s. By that time, Tony was dead and I sometimes wonder if his personal despair at the changes in his native city did not play a part in his demise.

It does, of course, take a considerable mental effort to quantify in ones mind the changes of almost a century and especially those of the fast moving 20th century. In many ways, a photographic record tells the story more effectively than the printed word can ever do.

For the bald facts convey very little. In 1801 the population of Aberdeen was 26,992. In 1901 it registered 153,503. In 1881 the telephone service had been inaugurated. In 1894 electricity had been introduced. In 1899 the first electric tram had run to Woodside. In 1914 the Gas Department introduced vertical retorts on the continuous carbonisation system, the first city in Scotland to so do. Clearly, progress was rapid and must have appeared startling to the late Victorian. Yet, mediaeval times were not far behind: the last public hanging in the Castlegate had taken place as recently as 1857 when the hapless John Booth was strung up before an approving audience for murdering his mother-in-law.

The year 1901 ushered in a new era with the death of Queen Victoria. Her death was a considerable loss to Aberdeen as her links with the City had been frequent and close — ever since Prince Albert's grand Scottish *schloss* had been erected at Balmoral and occupied after 1856. Many buildings in Aberdeen had been based on Balmoral out of a sort of homage to the Royals: Aberdeen Grammar School (1863), the Palace Hotel (1873), the Salvation Army Citadel (1896) and the General Post Office completed in 1906 (20). The South African War against the Boers was still being fought and the invincibility of the British Empire was in question for the first time. Social upheaval was in the wind as socialism, the Suffragettes and political reforms began to occupy the minds and hearts of the country's thinkers. But these were intellectual changes, difficult to quantify and to establish at a precise moment in time.

With the photograph changes can be instantly discerned. Changes in dress, transport, shops and places of work are all dramatically revealed by the photograph with very little effort of imagination required. I have a book, *Twenty One Aberdeen Events of the 19th Century*, which is, I suppose, a sort of 1912 predecessor of this book. There are stories of great fires, of disasters at sea, of Royal visits and appalling weather. All very much the sort of stuff the present reader will find in these pages. But what is very different about the nature of this book is that all these events of the present century are recorded by the medium of photography rather than the passage of purple prose. Whilst I would never subscribe to the dictum that the camera never lies (as it frequently does), I would, though, maintain that it is singularly effective in capturing a moment in time for later consideration. As every Picture Editor on any newspaper knows, a good picture is worth a thousand words and, researching this book, I have been looking for just that type of picture. The picture which does not simply and baldly portray some event but which tells us something more, whether in the gestures and expressions of those depicted, for example, or by their dress or actions, captured forever in a time capsule by the photographer. Photographs of buildings long gone are fascinating enough in themselves but, for me, pale into insignificance against the image of the Punch and Judy man on the beach (190) or the dancing couples at the Music Hall in the 1950s (176—7). These images capture people doing ordinary, everyday things all the more fascinating for coming from recent memory. Who can resist not looking again, closely, at the Circus Parade passing along Guild Street (185)? I know I can't as I smell again the animal dung and the greasepaint: a certain foretaste of pleasures to come. Thus, this becomes more than simply an interesting photograph.

I suppose that we call this nostalgia. But this is something of a pejorative term which seems to devalue its pursuit. We are all, for better or for worse, interested in where we came from and what happened in our own immediate area up to quite recent times. I don't think there is anything to be defensive about in this and, indeed, it can be construed as being indicative of a whole range of positive virtues from civic pride to family unity.

The photograph is a comparatively modern instrument of nostalgia and despite its present day accessibility has lost nothing of its charm or durability. Of course, the changes of this century have been so wide ranging that differences in building, transport, design, social activities and work are so marked as to make almost any old photograph instantly fascinating. This has made selection of images for this book something of a tricky exercise but some timeless criteria can be applied: do the pictures selected show something different or unusual which has changed now and do they say something about that process? The photographs of Patsy Gallagher (9) and "Foul Friday" (7), whilst comparatively recent, are locked as firmly in the past as a picture of the last public hanging would have been — had it been taken and survived. Similarly, the picture of the tired and emotional football supporter in Gothenburg (11) may simply be amusing to us today, but, in twenty or thirty years time, it will be a source of real fascination and, possibly, will stimulate theses and analyses outwith our present comprehension!

The photograph came early to Aberdeen and was far from being a new concept of vision in Aberdeen of the early 1900s. George Washington Wilson (1823—93), often referred to as Scotland's pioneer photographer, had settled in the city and, in 1840, began a notable career as artist and photographer. He took photographs not only of buildings and streets in Aberdeen, but also pictures of his fellow Aberdonians and the first ever picture of the moon. Some of his plates are now in the collection at Kings College of the University of Aberdeen. Many were owned by Tony Wyness (including that very first image of the moon): where they are now is a matter of mystery to those who knew him. Such early photographs are more redolent of the techniques and composition of painting — then the more firmly established art form.

7. Aberdeen worthy "Foul Friday", the hot chestnut man with his barrow in the Castlegate in the 1930s.

Many of these early images of the 1900s are taken from Edwardian picture postcards. The picture postcard was introduced in 1894 and from 1902 the Post Office permitted the use of the divided back card which allowed all of the front to be used for the picture and both message and name and address to be written on the verso. Picture postcards then poured onto the market. They were far more widely used than they are today and filled many more functions than those of simply imparting greetings from the seaside.

Many firms used them as advertising material and correspondence cards (VII, 106). Photographs were still not widely used in newspapers and this was sometimes the only readily available means of obtaining a picture of a significant event. Just as in the 80s, photographs of royalty, royal visits, and weddings were popular. It is recorded that picture postcards of musical comedy star Gertie Millar were in such demand that photographs of her face were often superimposed on images of other women's bodies! She sued the publishers of the pirate cards and lost in a society where the place of woman was still, as yet, undefined.

Some cards were used quite simply for sending straightforward messages and news — and

considerably more reliably than today. All mail was, almost without exception, delivered within 24 hours and, within the same area, often on the same day. Further comment would be superfluous!

Then there were the comic cards like those on page X cynically commenting upon the alleged propensity of the Aberdonian to meanness! During the 20s and 30s these were particularly popular. As the postcard craze caught on, people began to collect the cards in series and it became a most popular hobby as manufacturers dreamt up new series and subjects which could be circulated across the country for the price of a penny stamp. Many of the images were not strictly true to their subjects but reflected contemporary attitudes. "The rural working class was bathed in atmospheric haze for the aesthetic pleasures of the readers of *Country Life*" (Beckett & Cherry).

By the 20s the real postcard boom was over (some of the best had been printed in pre-First War Germany), social conditions had changed, the postage rate had doubled and the golden age of the postcard was over.

The development of roll film made available snapshots and photography at home. Cameras, although still a substantial luxury item, were becoming available to the affluent middle classes who were now able to experiment outwith the confines of the formal group portrait. But, for the vast majority of people, photography was still an activity beyond their means or reach.

The postcard is most often connected with leisure activity and Aberdeen Beach and the recreation associated with it are well recorded thanks to the efforts of generations of postcard sellers. But, over the years, many perfectly ordinary everyday activities have gone unrecorded by either postcard or camera. That is why I was particularly pleased to discover among the glass plates at Aberdeen Journals images like those of the hula hoop competition (178), jiving at the Music Hall (176), the twisting competition (180—1) and rock and roll (177). For it is these activities, taken for granted at the time and participated in within relatively recent memory by tens of thousands of Aberdonians which have now become themselves living legends: part of a common shared experience for a generation.

This book is really of the "Gosh! I remember that!" variety. For reasons which psychologists are better able to explain, human beings find it satisfying and fulfilling to reminisce and be reminded of places and things experienced directly or third hand. So, to that activity this book is what the board and cards are to Trivial Pursuits. It is something to gather around and use as the basis of a well worn, tried and tested game.

The 20th century has been well chronicled, especially since the Second World War, as a result of the increased availability of camera and film. Today virtually everyone has a camera and has become a photographer — at least of sorts. Probably at least half of the film shot is wasted and a further half of that is promptly lost or disposed of once processed. Even comparatively recent decades, like the 50s and 60s, are quite inadequately recorded despite the widespread availability of camera and film. Private photographs of the family tend to survive. Press photographs of Great Events survive. But remarkably little else. Great archives of photographic plates have been destroyed rather than the space given up to retain them and prints and negatives by the thousand have ended up in the refuse bin. Next time you are taking a photograph of some perfectly ordinary activity — say, a dance, the aerobics class or the kids at the beach, just think how interesting that image may be to people fifty years hence.

The other type of image which is of enduring interest is the news photograph of a dramatic event. Fires and accidents imprint themselves on the psyche and they make outstanding subjects for the photographer. Blazes like those at Aberdeen Combworks (242), the Athenaeum (240) or the Nigg Brae tanker incident (132) are remembered for a long time after, whether or not they are actually experienced first hand or merely third hand through the media. The closeness of the City to the sea is more than a matter of physical proximity and trouble at sea (129, 133) and the activities of the Aberdeen lifeboat (42, 252—259) have consistently interested Aberdonians.

There have been frequent bouts of drama and excitement for Aberdonians during the course of this century, although the reader will not find all of them within the confines of these covers. The Second War years are not covered: they are dealt with in a separate book, *Aberdeen at War* (Press & Journal, 1987). The First War years failed to benefit from the attentions of the photographer and many quite dramatic events seem to have gone unrecorded. What, for example, could have been more dramatic than the sinking of H M S *Hawke* by German submarine within sight of the City and with the loss of 500 lives? I searched in vain for some old plate showing the landing of survivors at Aberdeen or the rescue efforts but, in an all too familiar story, if such had existed then it is no more, broken or discarded as having no further interest.

Then there are dramatic events which because in substance they happen in private, behind closed doors, only photograph in a limited way. Few events captured the imagination of local people as much as the infamous Garvie Trial in the late 1960s. The sensational outpourings in the court were eagerly devoured by newspaper readers. But this was primarily a word story rather than a picture story. Nevertheless, local journalists and photographers scoured the north east for collect pictures of the participants taken in happier days in various states of dress and undress (135, 7, 8).

Gradual change is also difficult to capture with the camera. The before and after picture of some great building suddenly torn down is easily achieved. The identification with the camera of changes in education, health and social conditions is considerably more difficult and does, inevitably, mean that a pictorial history of this nature tends to be deficient in just those areas although the reader will get the odd hint here and there with pictures of the building of the Castlehill flats (221) and the Ashgrove scheme (238). The technique required to chart these developments is an altogether more subtle one and is something for another volume. Some pictures stand on their own as compelling images, like those of Foresterhill nurses around the time of the opening of the hospital (99, 100) but they

8. Proving even a monkey can sell newspapers! A circus chimp hands out copies of the old "Weekly Journal" in a late 40s publicity stunt.

9. Patsy Gallacher, the newspaper vendor, August 1954, at his stance at the top of Bridge Street.

10. Union Street bus queue in the rain, November 1967.

do not actually tell us a great deal about the conditions of the time.

Many have eloquently sung the praises of Aberdeen but few perhaps as lyrically as John S Sutherland, couthy author of *Aberdeen and Twal Mile Roon,* published in 1923:

OH, do not think, dear Aberdeen, that fronts the great North Sea,
And nestles like huge diamond fair between the Don and Dee,
That while of twal mile roon' I've sung I have not eyes to see
The sweet, enchanting beauty that all eyes must see in thee.
To praise the lovely casket fair means not that we condemn
What it was meant but to enclose — the still more lovely gem.
And gem thou art beyond compare, for search we every land,
No city's beauty can like thine men's homage deep command.

You might say he fair liked the place . . .
The origin of the phrase "Aberdeen an' Twal Mile Roon" does not actually belong to Sutherland but to the Aberdeen artist James Cassie, the author of many oft repeated north east sayings as well as an accomplished late 19th century artist. Apparently, he was incensed whilst attending a dinner of Edinburgh and Glasgow artists who were hotly debating the relative merits of their home towns and their contributions to Scottish art. Eventually, Cassie, much irritated by this discussion broke in: "De'il the bit! There's Jamesone, Dyce and Philip — tak awa' Aberdeen an'twal mile roon an'far are ye?"

Aberdeen does have a quite distinct ability to evoke a loyalty and affection not only amongst those actually born and bred in the City, but also in the more itinerant of residents. It must be something more than the gleaming granite, the sharp morning air or the quite breathtaking panorama as you sweep down into the city from the south with, all of a sudden, this totally unexpected collection of sparkling buildings as far as the eye can see.

I sometimes wonder if the attraction is nothing more than the indisputable fact of life that all British cities seem to increase in their attractiveness in direct proportion to their distance from London. On that particular scale, Aberdeen has to rate at the very top! But it is a little more complex than that. The relative remoteness of the City has served it well. It has enabled it to remain fiercely independent and even aloof when necessary. The citizenry have managed to retain an integrity born of their isolation from the outside world, even through the pressures of the most hectic of the oil years. Industries and activities of one sort or another have come to Aberdeen over the years . . . and departed. From the export of stockings to Europe in the 17th and 18th centuries, to the age of the tea clippers, linen manufacture and the granite industry, the fishing industry, papermaking and the oil industry. All these industries have come and gone, to a greater or lesser extent, but the character of the Aberdonian and the intangible feel of the City have, I suspect, remained immutable above the tide of human events. Again, these are characteristics perhaps difficult to discern from a book of photographs but if you care to look carefully I would like to think that clues like the set of a jaw, the neatly trimmed moustache and the upright bearing can give us more than a hint: isolated and isolationist but cosmopolitan in international connections centuries before the arrival of that relative youngster the oil industry; measured and reserved in response at first bu warm and hospitable before long; matter of fact and dry of wit, sometimes seeming to border on cynicism but solid and reliable in judgement; and an apparent conservatism which belies remarkable regenerative qualities.

These are all facets of the Aberdonian, like the proverbial bright light shining in a naughty world.

11. Tired and emotional Dons supporter after victory in Gothenburg!

SELECT BIBLIOGRAPHY

Jane Beckett & Deborah Cherry: *The Edwardian Era*, Phaidon/Barbican, London, 1987

W A Brogden: *Aberdeen, an Illustrated Architectural Guide*, RIAS Edinburgh, 1986

Gavin Cargill: *Blockade '75*, Molendinar Press, Glasgow, 1976

Corporation of the City of Aberdeen: *The Diced Cap: The Story of Aberdeen City Police*, Aberdeen, 1972

James D Ferguson: *The Story of Aberdeen Airport 1934—84*, Scottish Airports, Glasgow, 1984

J A Henderson: *Twenty One Aberdeen Events of the 19th Century*, The Daily Journal, Aberdeen, 1912

C. W. Hill: *Edwardian Scotland*, Scottish Academic Press, Edinburgh, 1976

Alexander Keith: *A Thousand Years of Aberdeen*, AUP, Aberdeen, 1972

J H Littlejohn: *Aberdeen Tivoli*, Rainbow Books, Aberdeen, 1986

W Mackie: *A Century of Craftsmanship — Alexander Hall & Son (Builders) Ltd. 1880—1980*, Mearns & Gill, Aberdeen, n. d.

John R Turner: *Scotland's North Sea Gateway, Aberdeen Harbour 1136—1986*, AUP, Aberdeen, 1986

Fenton Wyness: *Aberdeen Century of Change*, Impulse Publications, Aberdeen, 1971

Fenton Wyness: *City by the Grey North Sea*, Impulse Publications, Aberdeen, 1972

Newspaper files: *The Press & Journal, Evening Express* and *Bon Accord.*

12.   The coffee stall in the Castlegate was an institution for shift workers and late night revellers until closed by order of the magistrates in 1936. Its loss was mourned by nocturnal searchers after tea, coffee, Oxo, cigarettes and sweets.

13. Friday in the Castlegate, 1900.

14.   Boating on the Dee in Edwardian Times.

15.   The *Aberdeen Free Press* Building in Union Street, 1900. The *Free Press* moved there in 1895 from Broad Street. It now houses Esslemont & Mackintosh.

16. The Union Terrace corner, September 27th 1906. Flowers and flags celebrated Aberdeen University's 400th anniversary celebrations on the day King Edward VII opened the extension to Marischal College. The city celebrated for four days with decorations, illuminations, balls and receptions.

17. The Union Terrace junction with Union Street, circa 1900. The building to the left flying the flag was Mann's Grand Hotel, opened in 1892 by Charles Mann. Overlooked by the statue of Albert, the Prince Consort, is a horse drawn hackney carriage with the Rosemount tram in the middle distance. The statue was moved in 1913 to make way for that of King Edward VI

18.   Fresh milk is served in Midstocket Road, 1900.

19.   Market day in the Green, 1900. Fishwives and farmers vied for space to sell their wares. The lead statue of the "Mannie in the Green" was installed there in 1852 (from the Castlegate) and was moved again in 1958 — landing up eventually (1972) in the Castlegate again! The first piped water in the city was brought from a spring to "The Mannie" in 1706, in the Castlegate, before he started his travels!

21. *Above:* Crown Street at the turn of the century. The block of houses on the right was demolished to make way for the construction of the new General Post Office, opened by the Postmaster General in April, 1907.

20. *Left:* Aberdeen GPO, Crown Street, by W. T. Oldrieve (designer J. Cumming Wyness). The building with its Scots baronial features, contrasted pleasingly with the simpler granite buildings opposite.

22. Edwardian ladies, Castle Street, 1900.

23.   Posing for the photographers, the workers on the extensions to Union Bridge in 1905.

24.   The widened Union Bridge was opened in 1906.

25. Aberdeen Harbour at the turn of the century. Photographed by George Washington Wilson from the tower of the Town House.

26. These Edwardian sunbathers are somewhat overdressed by our standards of today. The bathing station lies behind the beach.

27.   The Aberdeen Harbour Ferry, around 1910.

28.   A line of Kirkcaldy registered herring drifters entering the harbour circa. 1910 to land their catches at the Fishmarket.

29. The harbour pictured in the sunlight of early morning.

SUNLIT WATERS,
THE DOCKS.
ABERDEEN.

1482.

30. An Edwardien postcard view of the launch of the S. S. "Intaba", September 6th 1910. At the time she was the largest vessel ever built in Aberdeen at 401 feet long and 4,700 tons deadweight.

31. Early morning in the fish market, 1910.

FISH MARKET, ABERDEEN 137

32. Union Street shortly before the First War. Trams, bicycles, horses and cars are competing for space! To the left is the Forsyth Hotel, later the Gloucester.

33. The New Market, 1905.

34. The widened Union Bridge, 1910, with His Majesty's Theatre (completed in 1906) in the background.

35. Boer War Parade at Queen's Cross, 1902. The house on the corner was the home and studio of pioneer Aberdeen photographer George Washington Wilson.

36. John Smart advertised a "Car to carry 14 passengers any distance for picnics, cricket, golf or football teams. Wednesday, Saturday and Sunday excursions". He operated from Beechgrove House, now the headquarters of the BBC in Aberdeen and sold to then in the 30s by architect Tom Scott Sutherland.

37. Clark's Lane.

38. Jack's Brae in the Gilcomston area: now gone.

39. These two photographs graphically illustrate the social divides at the turn of the century. *Above,* fishwives make their way to work.

40. Edwardian lady cyclists at the Beach Boulevard.

41. King Street Fire Station around 1900. The purpose-built station was opened on May 31st 1899 by Baillie Lyon. It was manned by a firemaster, deputy firemaster, 11 full-time and 10 auxiliary firemen. The fire engines were pulled by horses at that time. There was still a horse-drawn fire engine in use in the 1920s.

42. Launching the old Aberdeen lifeboat *Bon Accord* from the beach at the turn of the century. She then had to be rowed to the assistance of the casualty.

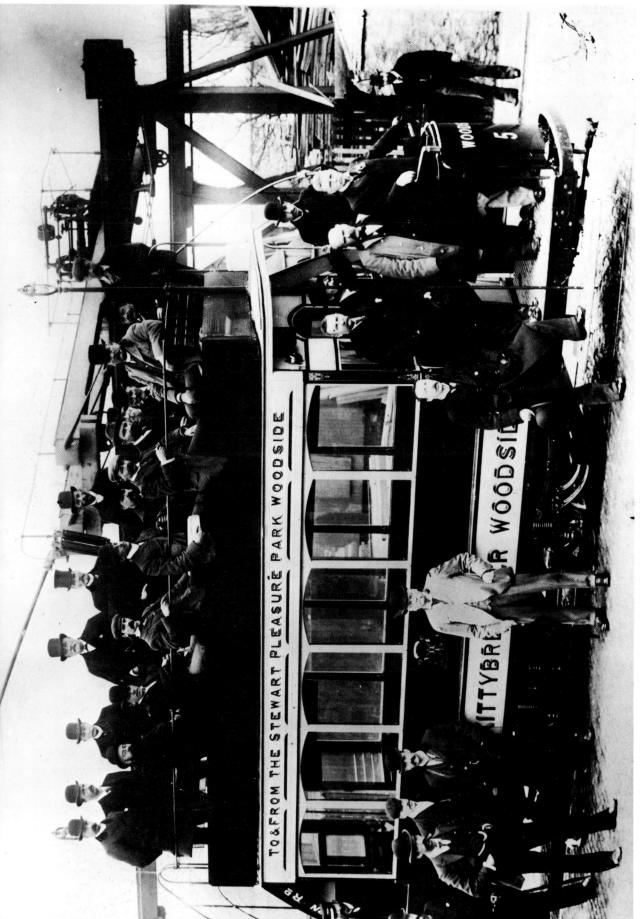

43.   The opening of the first electric tram service in George Street, December 22nd 1898.

44. Learning to handle the bicycle. A bold Edwardian lady tackles the mysteries of machinery in Riverside Drive in the early 1900s.

45. Perhaps Sir Clive Sinclair had this in mind
when he designed his ill-fated C 5 motor
car!

6. A Landau carriage passes Woolworths on
Union Street, the first multiple in the city
opened 1914, where the sign boldly
declares, "Nothing over sixpence"!

47. Two Aberdonians with their brand new 1907 Argyll Tourer, a Scottish manufactured car made at Alexandria, Dunbartonshire.

48. Mr. Simpson with his new car.

49. A splendid array of motors in this Union Row garage before the First War. For the purposes of the photograph the chauffeur has been Note the "modesty boards" installed on the stairs to the upper deck lest ladies be obliged to display a little too much leg.

50. Electric trams were first introduced in Aberdeen, on the Woodside route, in 1899 and all the routes were electrified by mid-1902. Then horse-drawn trams were withdrawn. This historic photographs shows the Rosemount tram (circular route by Queen's Cross, Rosemount and Union Terrace), drawn by a pair of sturdy greys, alongside an electrified trum running to Mannofield. This picture was taken in 1901. Note the "modesty boards" installed on the stairs to the upper deck lest ladies be obliged to display a little too much leg.

51. Car No 2 on the Woodside route.

1900

52. Car No 29, an open-cab electric, at the Bayview Road terminus, 1906 (routing Castle Street, Albyn Place and Queen's Road).

53. Water tram car, circa 1912, cleaning the streets.

54. Lady conductresses are now on the trams.
    Jeanette McLeod pictured aboard No 14,
    Bridge of Dee bound, in the early 1920s.

55. Pigs on the run from the market in
    Kittybrewster seem unconcerned by the
    Market Street bound tram in this
    photograph from the 1950s.

56. The Castlegate, 1936, with open-fronted tramcar No 79, running from Hazlehead, negotiating the points at the King Street junction. Note the lamp at both sides of the destination screen. After the Second War illumination was provided by one single, square lamp box.

57. Salting the points at Bridge of Don.

58. Tram terminus on Fountainhall Road at Queen's Cross. Now the site of Grampian TV Studios, opened 1961.

59. Queen's Cross, 1937.

60. A well wooded Albyn Place, complete with iron railings removed in the Second War.

61.　Trams and buses in Union Street, 1950.

62.　Tram cars in King Street, 1953.

63.　The last tram to Woodside, November 19th 1955.

64. Bluebird buses parked in Upper Denburn Road, 1960, before the bus station was built.

65. A motor bus at the beach in the 1920s.

66. The Cruden Bay bus negotiates a somewhat narrower Bridge of Don, March 1952.

67. This Aberdeen Corporation bus, a Daimler CVD 6 delivered in 1947, was bought by a Dutch pirate radio station and became Holland's only double decker bus. It is pictured here in 1970 in front of the Royal Palace, Dam Square, Amsterdam. It later returned to Aberdeen but was eventually scrapped. The engine, though, ended up in an Aberdeen fishing boat.

68. *Top left:* The opening of Dyce Aerodrome, July 28th 1934 by Lord Arbuthnott (left). The moving force behind the 'drome was Eric Gandar Dower (right).

69. Seven passengers who made the first Orkney-Aberdeen flight at Dyce Airport, May 28th, 1935. The flight took just over two hours and there was intense competition between Gandar Dower's Aberdeen Airways Service and Kintore-based Highland Airways.

70. Sunderland flying boat in Aberdeen Harbour.

71. *Above:* The sail training ship Gorch Foche in the Harbour, 1959.

72. *Right:* The Aberdeen holiday, July 1950, produces crowds at the station which are now but a memory. In the background is the fine wooden bookstall (now removed) and the "Telegraph Office".

73. *Right:* The Joint Station, August 1938.

74. The old Schoolhill Station, at the side of His Majesty's Theatre, now demolished.

75. Aberdeen Joint Station suburban platforms at the south east corner of Bridge Street, completed 1920, from where trains ran to Deeside and Buchan. Note the gas lamps, fruit stall and advertisement boards.

76. The last train from Aberdeen to Ballater, February 27th 1966.

77. The steam train *Bon Accord* at the station, 1974.

78. The Aberdeen *Press & Journal* offices in Broad Street in the 1920s.

79. *Top right:* Preparing the matrixes.

80. *Right:* The print room.

81. *Below:* The wire room at Broad Street, 1948. Here photographs were sent and received and the teleprinters were operated. Nowadays, the modern equivalent of all this hardware would sit on top of one desk!

82. P & J despatch staff, 1920s.

85. When Aberdeen Journals new offices and plant at Mastrick were being constructed this "newshound", named Rover by his adopted owners, roamed around the site and was adopted as the Journals offical pet. He is seen here with compositor Dennis Fraser and the then features writer Ranald Allan (1970).

83. May 1979 and the last paper is set by traditional hot metal techniques.

84. The old Linotype ("hot metal") setting machines — a world away from direct input computers.

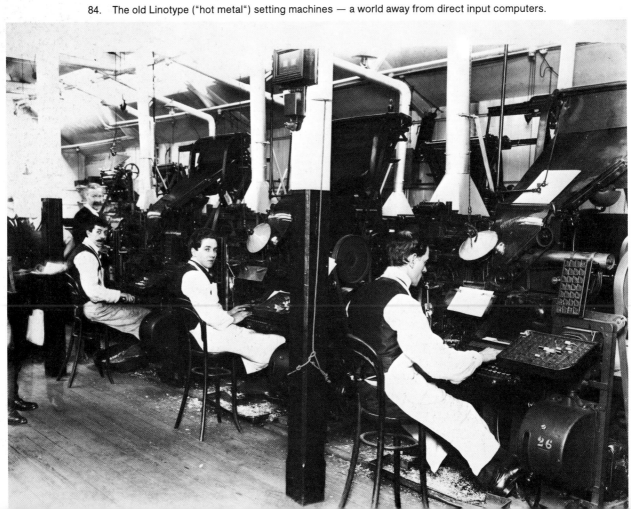

86. At the gates of the Hall Russell Yard in the early 1950s.

87. Launch of M. V. *Thameshaven* from Hall Russells, January 1971. Built for Havenlijn of Rotterdam it is, at 10,500 tons, the largest ship to be built in Aberdeen.

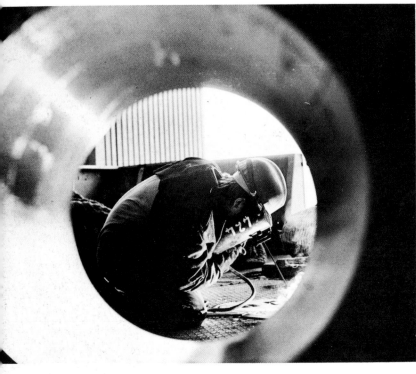

88. Welder Mike McCann working on the Navy ship *Salmoor*, launched May 1985.

89. *Bottom left:* In the 370ft. long dry dock at Hall Russell & Co., the Orkney Islands Shipping Co. trader *Islander* undergoing a refit (July 1975).

90. Unloading herring at Torry, 1964.

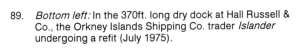

91. Shortly before the First War, the wooden-hulled paddle tug *Granite City* tows a line of Kircaldy fishing boats up the Navigation Channel into the harbour to land their catches at the Fish Market.

92. January 1953 and the fishing industry is going strong: trawlers crammed into the harbour as far as the eye can see.

93. A catch of herring waits to b
    loaded onto lorries bound fo
    the curer's yard, March 194

94. Gutting fish at Aberdeen Fis
    Market, 1946.

95. Devanha Brewery employees dressed up for their annual outing.

6. Brewery drays in Virginia Street, 1937.

97. Beer bottling at Devanha Brewery, 1942.

98. Aberdeen Royal Infirmary, Foresterhill, under construction in 1935.

99. Classes for nurses at Foresterhill, June 1936.

100. Nurses lined up outside the new Infirmary on official opening day, September 24th, 1936. The infirmary was opened by the Duke of York, accompanied by his wife, the Queen Mother. (King Edward VIII was unable to make it due to distractions esewhere).

101.   Tailors at Loch Street Co-op Works in what looks suspiciously like Chinese style sweat shop conditions

103. Working in Rubislaw Quarry at the turn of the century.

104. Probably the most famous charity stunt by Aberdeen students was the suspension of a banner across Rubislaw Quarry in April 1966.

102. In its day, perhaps the most famous hole in the ground in the world: certainly the deepest. Rubislaw Quarry was in production for almost 200 years and was 480 feet deep, 900 foot long and 750 feet wide.

105. The buildings at the foot of the man-made quarry before it was closed in 1971.

106. An Edwardian picture postcard features the granite works of James Taggart at 92 Great Western Road.

107.   The 130th Birthday Celebration Sale, at the Equitable, St. Nicholas Street, May 1966. Every 130th customer who left the store received a free birthday cake.

108.   A survivor of the retail revolutions of the 20th century, the Esslemont & Mackintosh store in Union Street.

109.   The George Street branch of Alexanders, the radio and cycle dealers.

110.   *Bottom left:* The drapery department at the old Northern Cooperative Society shop in George Street (now replaced by Norco House).

111.   The Market Arcade outside the New Market entrance in the early 1930s.

112.   Well known local author and historian, Fenton Wyness signs copies of *Spots from the Leopard* in the old Watt & Grant bookshop in Union Street in 1971. Looking on are Securicor men (in charge of the solid gold pen) and purchasers Ruth Mitchell, Penny Bellamy and Linda Clark.

113.   60th Anniversary Sale of Isaac Benzies, 1954, and a welcome cuppa for early bargain hunters. Isaac Benzie set up in business in 1894 and by 1906 had 7 branches. By 1934 activities were centralised in the George Street branch and the store became part of Arnotts in 1973.

114.   Fresh fish and vegetables on sale in the Castlegate Market during the 1930s.

115.   The old John Jackson garage at the corner of Justice Mill Lane and Bon Accord Street, circa 1935, with the stocks laid out for public view. Mr. Jackson displayed the very first motor car in Aberdeen in the late 1890s.

116.   Inside Ogston & Tennant's Gallowgate soap factory.

117.   The staff of His Majesty's Theatre during the 1920s.

118.   Checking penny in the slot gas meters, 1935.

119.   The Castlegate Market on a Saturday in 1935. Note the stall is lit by a paraffin flare.

120.   Threshing above the Dee within sight of the city (Kincorth to the right of the picture), 1966.

121.   Union Street is patrolled by mounted police during the
        General Strike of 1926.

122.   In the 1960s, student Charities Week stunts were
        frequently outrageous and gained a good deal of press
        publicity. In those rather more relaxed days, they
        frequently involved the liberal use of firearms. In 1968,
        several students were arrested and prosecuted for
        staging a mock gangland killing on the steps of a Union
        Street cinema. In this incident, a hostage was taken in
        the shape of well known local Liberal party activist
        Nigel Lindsay.

123. The aftermath of the great snowstorm of December 1908 which paralysed the city Over 700 men worked to clear the snow in the centre of the city. Here snow is cleared in Union Street. The city was cut off by road, rail and telegraph. The tramway system was forced to a halt by waist high drifts.

124. Clearing the Buchan line near Aberdeen, December 1908. Many trains were marooned after days of continuous snow at the end of the month.

CLEARING THE BUCHAN LINE NEAR ABERDEEN.

125. Stranded vehicles in the snow on the Aberdeen-Kintore road, January 1960.

126.   Struggling with the snow in Union Street, 1942.

127.   In the summer of 1930 the enormous German airship *Graf Zeppelin* flew over Aberdeen en route home after a Scandinavian cruise. It occasioned general panic and amazement as thousands of people poured onto the streets and all traffic was brought to a standstill.

128.   The fishermens' blockade of 1975 which threatened to close the harbour completely. Here the blockade is run by the *St. Clair*. Protesting inshore fishermen banded together and took unprecedented action in protest against economic conditions in the industry which threatened them with ruin.

129.   A dramatic photograph taken in March 1969 as a trawler rounds the south breakwater of Aberdeen Harbour in heavy seas.

130.   The old Northern Hotel at Kittybrewster was destroyed by fire in April 1938. Built about 1880 in baronial style, it drew much of its trade from farmers attending the Mart and travellers using Kittybrewster railway station.

131.   On the night of October 31st, 1941 the Palace Hotel, at the corner of Union Street and Bridge Street, caught fire and was completely gutted in one of Aberdeen's most dramatic blazes.

132.   This butane gas tanker, burned "like a great incendiary bomb" for 36 hours with flames shooting 100 feet into the air at Nigg Brae, January 1974.

133.   The polish trawler *Nurzic* ashore at Balmedie in January 1974.

134. The Garvie trial brought enormous queues for seats in the courtroom as sensation piled on sensation with tales of sexual perversion, nudism, pornographic photographs and a "kinky cottage".

135. The Garvie murder trial rocked and scandalised Aberdeen in December 1968. At the High Court in the city, Sheila Garvie, an attractive 34-year-old blonde was sentenced to life imprisonment for the murder of her wealthy farmer husband, along with her 22-year-old lover, Brian Tevendale. The duo are pictured above.

136.   Much of the hostility of the crowd was directed against Crown witness Trudy Birse, the dead man's lover, who told the court of his incredible sexual demands which she claimed to be able to satisfy.

137.   Maxwell Garvie, murder victim, photographed with his wife, Sheila, in October, 1965.

139.   Prison for life to Sheila Garvie (hooded) and her former lover (on the steps).

38.   A photograph taken of Maxwell Garvie and his wife, Sheila, at
the infamous so-called "Kinky Cottage" where Max Garvie set
up his own private nudist colony.

140.   The last man in Scotland to be hanged for murder was Henry Burnett at one minute past eight in the morning on August 15th, 1963. He was hanged at Craiginches Prison. A grim looking crowd waits outside the prison.

141.   One of Aberdeen's great unsolved murder mysteries was the Betty Hadden case in 1945. Only her forearm and hand were found on the south foreshore of the harbour navigation channel. The rest of her body was never found.

142. There was worldwide - unlooked for - notoriety for Aberdeen in the early summer of 1964 when an 11lb can of corned beef from a supermarket in the city sparked off the disastrous typhoid outbreak. The spread was rapid and dramatic. The Medical Officer of Health for Aberdeen, Dr. Ian MacQueen became something of a celebrity as he faced the press and television daily throughout the crisis. To his right is seated the late Charles Easton, local boss of D.C. Thomsons, and one of the city's best known journalists.

143. Even the swings were closed!

144. Friends and relatives were obliged to stay outside when visiting the City Hospital.

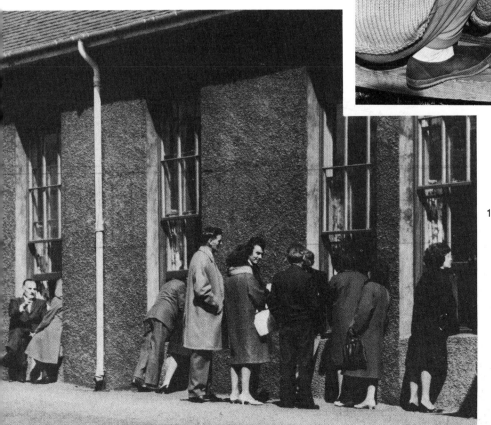

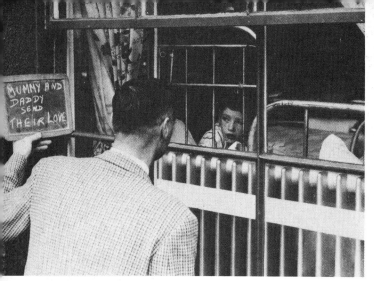

145. This is the picture which really said it all. Published all over the world and exhibited internationally, this photograph epitomised the isolation that typhoid brought to Aberdeen.

146. The official "all clear" was sounded when H. M. The Queen visited the city after the outbreak.

147. The Queen was greeted by enormous crowds.

148.   The Dons win the 1947 Scottish Cup Final with the scoreline Hibs 1, Aberdeen 2. The cup is held high by skipper Frank Dunlop.
Left to right: Taylor, McCall, McKenna, Hamilton, McLaughlin,, Williams, Harris, Waddell and William Mitchell, club chairman.

149.   Players' wives and girlfriends off to the 1970 Cup
Final. The Scottish Cup was brought home by the
Dons.

150. The 1982 Cup Final brought the scoreline Aberdeen 4, Rangers 1, after extra-time. Here Mark McGhee's header sails past the outstretched arm of Rangers keeper Stewart for the Dons second goal.

151. The 1983 Cup in the bag as well . . . Skipper Willie Miller holds the Scottish Cup aloft at Hampden.

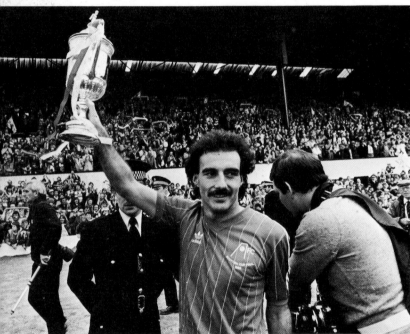

153. John Hewitt jumps for joy after scoring the winning goal in the European Cup-Winners' Cup, May 1983, Gothenburg.

152. The 1986 Cup was captured 3:0 against Hearts. Hampden scorers John Hewitt and Billy Stark on the balcony on the Town House with manager Alex Ferguson and Lord Provost Henry Rae.

154. Two days after the match the special boatload of fans arrive back at Aberdeen Harbour aboard the *St. Clair*. Manager Alex Ferguson and Mark McGhee greeted them.

155.   Aberdeen Ladies Football Club, 1921.

156.   The first Aberdeen Girls' Hiking Club outing.

157.   Party at the Y.W.C.A., Broad Street, in 1926.

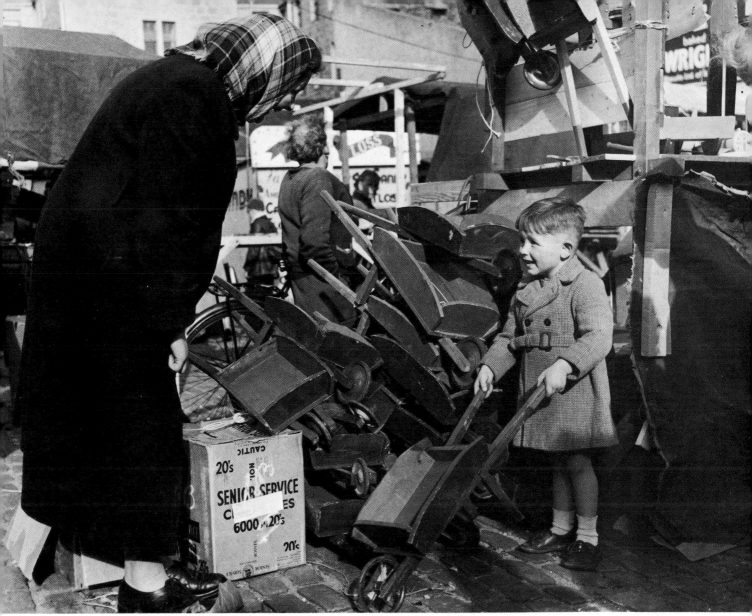

158.   Three-year-old Robert Henderson tries a wooden barrow for size at the August 1956 Timmer Market. Today plastic toys and cheap jewellery have supplanted the finely crafted wooden articles. It is now held in the Justice Street car park.

9.   The centuries old Timmer Market, August 30th, 1945, in the Castlegate. Traditionally, wooden goods of every type were available from peashooters and mouse-traps to washtubs and tattie choppers.

160. *Right:* The old Playhouse Cinema, 483 Princes Street. Redeveloped.

161. *Below:* The Astoria, Kittybrewster, is demolished, April 1967.

162. The Casino Cinema, Wales Street. Opened 1916, closed 1959.

163. The Belmont Cinema. Opened 1936, closed 1952.

164. The Astoria Cinema, with its art deco facade, opened in 1934.

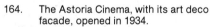

165. The Majestic. Closed 1973 and site in Union Street redeveloped as shops and offices.

166. The Palace Cinema in 1959. Built for circus use, converted to a cinema by the Pooles, later a dance hall, now a disco.

167. *Below:* Torry cinema, Crombie Road, in 1966. Opened 1921, closed 1968.

168. The Gaumont in 1957 attracts a queue of eager cinemagoers. Construction started in the late 1930s but was interrupted by the war. It was completed in 1954 and opened as the Regal.

169. The Grand Central Cinema, George Street, opened by the Donalds in 1930 and closed October 17th, 1981.

170. The Frigate Bar, Netherkirkgate, in the 1930s with smartly turned out bar staff.

171. A gleaming Criterion Bar in the 1930s. This Guild Street bar was traditionally popular with Tivoli patrons who doubtless appreciated the polished wood and brass taps.

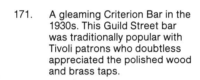

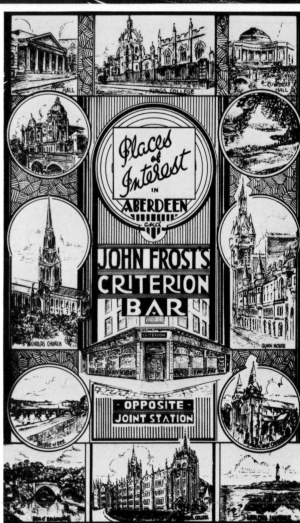

173. A legend in its own lifetime, the Palais Ballroom, starting point for so many Aberdeen romances.

172. A postcard advertising the Criterion Bar in its heyday.

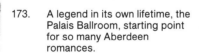

174. A feature of life until comparatively recently — the tearoom. Pictured here is the Loch Street Arcade tearoom in the 30s.

75. Tommy Steele appeared at the Capitol in 1957.

76. Jiving the night away, the Music Hall, 1951.

177. Rock 'n' Roll takes grip, 1956.

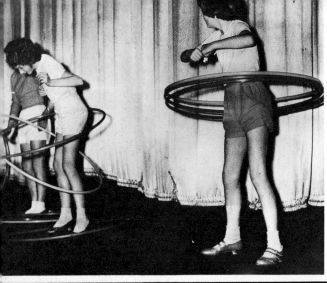

178. The hula hoop craze, 1958. A competition in progress at The Odeon.

179. The audience at the Capitol, 1964. The Capitol was opened as a cinema by Bert Gates in 1933 and was one of the best in the country. In 1941 it was sold to the Donalds.

180. Twisting Competition in 1962 as another dance craze takes root.

181. A young competitor takes a breather. Note the interesting contemporary fashion in dress.

182. Go-Go Girls at the Place Discotheque, Rose Street, 1966.

183. Aberdeen's first mobile disco, The Four Knights of the Round Table, at the University, 1968. In the foreground, publicity girls Pat Gebhardt (left) and Jacqui Powell.

184. The Miss Press & Journal contest, 1974. The winner was Patricia McWilliam of Cairnie who was obviously taken aback at the announcement.

185.
Now gone forever, the popular circus parades. This was for Billy Smart's Circus visit of June, 1966. The photograph was taken in Guild Street.

186.   Girls bathing in the 1950s.

187.   Well dressed for the beach in the 1930s.

188. On the scenic railway in the 30s.

189. The amusement park at Aberdeen beach in 1937. Most popular was the scenic railway built by American showman John Henry Iles. It was burned down on December 5th, 1940.

190. The Punch & Judy man on the beach, July 1939.

191. Vintage style dodgems, 1937.

193. Sunday afternoon entertainment on Aberdeen Links, 1933. Seats were 2d a time to listen to the brass band, but you could stand for free — hence the large audience outside the railings. Apparently, most of the standing audience usually disappeared before two of the bandsmen took a collection outside the railings!

192. A picture taken in 1936 of the First War tank which was an attraction on the Broad Hill for families spending a raised a staggering £15 million for Defence Bonds when the tank 'Julian' arrived in the city.

The last show at the Tivoli Theatre, September 28th, 1963. Calum Kennedy (centre), the Joe Gordon Folk Four and Irene Campbell and the Heatherisle Dancers are on stage for the final curtain.

Victory signs all round. Will Fyfe and Harry Gordon after their concert at the NAAFI, Market Street, on VE Day, 1945. Between the two comics is Lord Provost Tommy Mitchell.

196. Horse racing at Seaton Park, June 1937.

197. Speedboat trips around Aberdeen Bay were a feature of the facilities on offer at Aberdeen Beach during the 1950s.

198. A 1959 picture of well known local amateur TT rider Sid Barro at Aberdeen Harbour with his Buick motor car.

199. A Sunday afternoon out at the Bay of Nigg in 1934. Pre-war it was a popular spot for some relaxation on a Sunday afternoo

200. The Cowdray Hall takes shape in the early 20s.

201. The opening of Cowdray Hall, 1926.

202. A barefoot young urchin fights his way to the front of the crowd for a view!

203. Now gone, but once a mecca for bargain hunters, Alex ("Cocky") Hunter's stores in Castle Terrace. "Cocky" Hunter would buy or sell virtually anything, although general tidiness was not a feature of his emporium.

204. One of the last Aberdeen milk carts photographed in Woodside.

205. Demolition of buildings in Broad Street at the turn of the century. Marischal College now stands on this site. Lord Byron was one of the street's more famous residents.

206. The western end of Queen Street in the 60s, shortly before demolition.

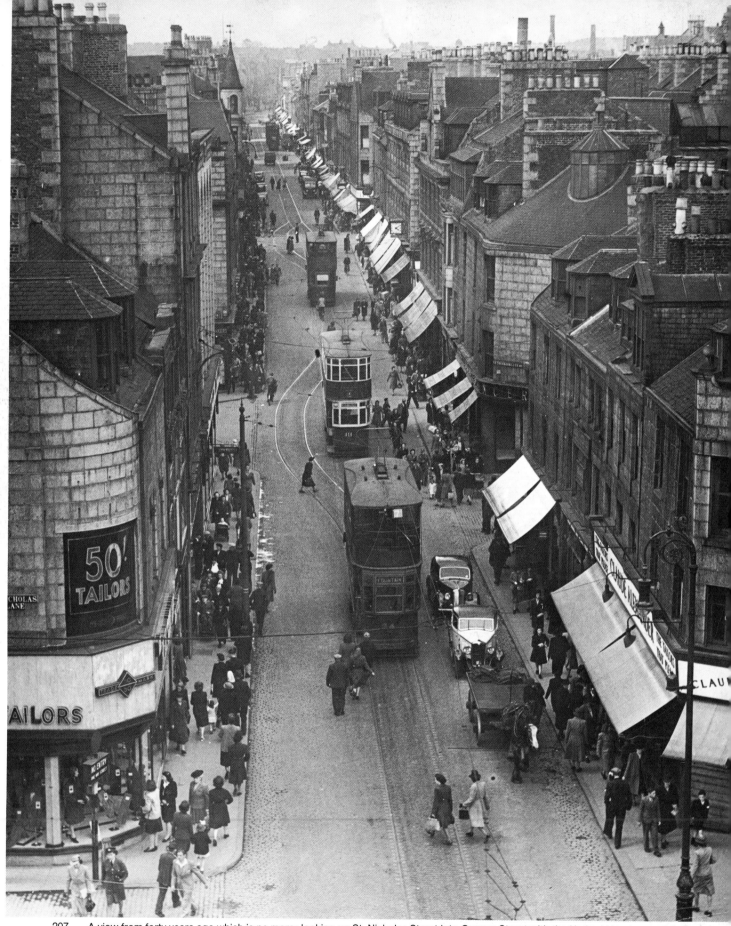

207. A view from forty years ago which is no more: looking up St. Nicholas Street into George Street with the Netherkirkgate opening the first on the right and Correction Wynd the first on the left.

208. George Street and St. Nicholas Street looking towards Upperkirkgate in the days before the St. Nicholas Centre was ever dreamt of. The famous watch at Kemp the jewellers shows the time (as it did for years) at 7.21. Birnies site was later taken over by the Rubber Shop.

209. Property, now demolished, in Gerrard Street looking from the Gallowgate. Here, one of the first family planning clinics in Britain was set up.

211. The Well of Spa Bar demolished in the development of the Denburn Health Centre.

210. A 1957 picture of the Gallowgate/Littlejohn Street corner, now demolished. Note the granite setts. All that is now left are the Marischal College railings on the right!

212. The Denburn area in 1956. To the right, the Upper Denburn is being demolished and all the other buildings in foreground and middleground are doomed. Gas lamps and granite setts are still in evidence. A bus station was planned for this site but the scheme was abandoned and the bus station built instead in Guild Street.

213. The Guestrow slum clearance area, looking from Broad Street through Blairton Lane towards Guestrow.

214. The Shoe Lane slum clearance area, at the back of Marischal College, looking towards West North Street.

215. A 1932 postcard view of Mounthooly-Causewayend junction at the foot of the Gallowgate.

16. A 1970 aerial view from the top of Gallowgate flats of a small Mounthooly roundabout which was considerably enlarged to its present size bringing the destruction of most of the surrounding buildings.

217. A decrepit looking Provost Ross's House (1593) in the Shiprow in a picture taken in early 50s. It was restored in 1953.

218. Further up the Shiprow, charming old buildings which were soon to disappear in favour of a multi-storey car park and shopping development for Grandfare to the right and the ABC Cinema development to the left.

219. Old Aberdeen Post Office in the 1950s.

Gordon Highlanders march from Castlehill Barracks for the last time in August 1935. Erected in 1794, the Barracks were demolished in 1965 to make way for the Castlehill flats. The Gordon Highlanders removed to Bridge of Don.

A 1967 picture of the erection of the multi-storey Castlehill flats. During the 19th century the grassy banks sloping down to Commerce Street were used as bleachgreens.

222. A 1930s picture of the Palace Hotel, burned out in the War, and eventually replaced by the C & A department store.

223. The old Northern Club premises at the corner of Union Street and Huntly Street, pictured in 1962. This handsome building was demolished in 1963 to make way for a shopping development.

24. The Wallace Tower in the Netherkirkgate was demolished in 1964 to make way for Marks & Spencer's. It was, however, carefully rebuilt at Tillydrone and local historian Dr. W. Douglas Simpson lived there until his death in 1968.

25. The old Northern Co-operative Society Headquarters.

26. The derelict and deserted Co-op arcade pictured in the early 80s after 15 years of neglect. Demolished as part of the Bredero development.

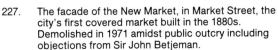

227. The facade of the New Market, in Market Street, the city's first covered market built in the 1880s. Demolished in 1971 amidst public outcry including objections from Sir John Betjeman.

228. Seaton House, built circa 1725 to designs by James Gibbs, was destroyed by fire in 1963 whilst in the ownership of the Corporation who were considering its future.

229. The Winter Gardens, Duthie Park, are demolished, May 1969, after the roof was damaged in a gale. It was built 1899—1900 in St. Petersburg redwood, glazed with sheetglass, with hot water pipes for the heating — all for £1,550!

230. 18th century Burnside House on Westburn Road, demolished for housing.

231. The tripod shear poles at Waterloo Quay, used since the turn of the century for lifting heavy machinery and ships' boilers, are brought down early one June morning, 1975.

232. The second widening of Union Bridge this century in 1963. The Bridge is widened to accommodate a row of shops on the near side.

233. The widening of the bridge and road at Bridge of Don, 1958.

234.   Aberdeen Feeing market, Castlegate, 1935.

235.   The Feeing Market, 1938. The "loons" who failed to find a fee and farm work were eagerly seized upon by the army recruiting sergeants.

236. A busy Aberdeen Harbour in the 1980s as oil rig supply boats jostle for berths in Victoria Dock.

237. The Corn Market,
Hadden Street,
March 16th 1939.

238. Aberdeen's first
multi-storey flats
take shape in the
Ashgrove housing
scheme, March
1960.

239.   This was the first motorised fire appliance in Aberdeen, pictured with a proud firemaster standing before it.

240. Outside King Street fire station, 1922. Two appliances with (centre) Firemaster Bell, Deputy Firemaster McLaughlan and a visiting local councillor.

241. Second War appliances bearing National Fire Service insignia attend a tenement fire in the city.

242. There have been a number of serious fires at Aberdeen Combworks over the years. The April 1969 fire was one of the biggest in the city. This photograph was taken from the top of the Gallowgate flats.

243. Fire at Middleton's the printers in Rose Street, May 1968. Their paper store was destroyed. The former Rose Street printing works had been destroyed by fire in 1949.

244. The disastrous fire at the beautiful Royal Athenaeum Restaurant (1819), August 1973. Despite the proximity of the fire station in King Street, around the corner, the building was well alight when the brigade arrived.

245.   An RAF fire crew in action at a chimney blaze at Aboyne Road, Garthdee, November 1977.

246.   During the firemens' strike of 1977—78 the armed services were called in and the old Green Goddess fire engines were trundled out of mothballs. Here two RAF men practice with a hose at Bridge of Don barracks.

247.   Saved! The Scottish Cup, won by the Dons in 1970, is rescued by firemen from the Pittodrie blaze, February 1971. Much of the main stand and offices were gutted by the fire.

248.   The spectacular blaze at Aberdeen Grammar School, July 1986. Lord Byron looks on . . .

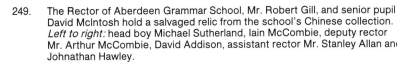

249. The Rector of Aberdeen Grammar School, Mr. Robert Gill, and senior pupil David McIntosh hold a salvaged relic from the school's Chinese collection. *Left to right:* head boy Michael Sutherland, Iain McCombie, deputy rector Mr. Arthur McCombie, David Addison, assistant rector Mr. Stanley Allan and Johnathan Hawley.

250. Sixth year pupil Emily Maxfield tells her story to an *Evening Express* reporter at the blaze.

251. The blaze, which was started by a workman burning paint from a window, spread rapidly through the roof of the school.

252. The motor lifeboat in the Harbour
in the 1930s.

253. Launching the old beach lifeboat
Bon Accord.

254.   No.2 lifeboat lends assistance — inland — during the Maryculter floods of 1951.

255.   A caterpillar tractor assists in the launching of the *George and Elizabeth Gow*, Aberdeen's No.2 lifeboat, in April 1955.

256.   The *Grace Paterson Ritchie* pictured at Waterloo Quay upon delivery to Aberdeen, September 1966.

258.   Launch of a new inshore rescueboat at Balmedie by Councillor George Christie, June 1976.

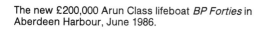
The new £200,000 Arun Class lifeboat *BP Forties* in Aberdeen Harbour, June 1986.

259.   Airyhall Primary 7 School pupils are shown round the new
Aberdeen lifeboat, May 1986.

260.   August 1985 and a rock climber is rescued from the cliffs at
Cove by Aberdeen Coastguard Rescue Company.

261. At the end of October 1966 Aberdeen University's new Zoology Building collapsed whilst under construction and fell to the ground just like the proverbial deck of cards. Despite a massive rescue operation, five men died in the disaster.

262. *Inset*: The partially completed Zoology Building pictured just before the disaster.

263.   A contretemps with the long arm of the law is depicted in this 1936 photograph.
"Fat are ye daen loons?"
"Naethin!"

264.   "Here's tae us, Wha's like us!" Cake made to celebrate
the 200th birthday of The Press & Journal in 1948.